About Thomas Farber's Terses, Teases, Means & Extremes

Truth be Told does more than compact the world into the essence perceived by its idiosyncratic compositor. It also hints at an expansive hidden narrative of sex, death, joy and despair. In short, as the author presumably prefers all things, it may be an epigramasterpiece.

—Melvin Jules Bukiet, *A Faker's Dozen*

The strategy of most literary compression is to stringently focus the reader's attention, even confine it, to the writer's carefully controlled meanings. Tom Farber's alchemical epigrams, however, manage to achieve a counterintuitive opposite. Through juxtaposition, cadence, surprise—balancing acts of extreme delicacy—Farber's dialectical word-craft offers space for the reader's imagination and helps it roam through possibilities. His gift is not spareness but, with a wry smile, a gentle prod toward plenitude.

—Joseph Matthews, *The Lawyer Who Blew Up His Desk*

In Farber's work, sense is sharply halted, turned upside down, then sent weaving off in a giddy new direction. It's a master act of crazy balance and performative wit, every thought "riddled with perfection."

—Cathy Luchetti, *Women of the West*

Every epigram in *Hesitation Marks* is a surprise, a little jolt, a stab of wit. Farber exposes truths behind human behavior by playing with language, daringly juggling such themes as aging, hypocrisy, betrayal, envy. These epigrams offer little comfort, except in their originality and skillful compression they almost transcend themselves.

—Olivia Dresher, *In Pieces: An Anthology of Fragmentary Writing*

Tom Farber casts an incisive eye on a potent range of subjects that touch our lives: sexuality, intimacy, marriage, divorce, old age, money, class, justice. In these pithy statements, far more complex than they appear, he marries psychological insight with word play and wit with gravity...

—Susan Griffin, *Wrestling with the Angel of Democracy*

If Dr. Johnson, Ambrose Bierce, and Dorothy Parker had a literary three-way, [Farber's] epigrams would be a suitable love child...

—Scott Hulet, Editor, *The Surfer's Journal*

Farber crams a lot into his own sayings…Many are miniature novellas—a glimpse of some hinted-at encounter, a one-sided dialogue with characters only known as 'he' or 'she'...

—James Geary, *Geary's Guide to the World's Great Aphorists*

If quantity makes quality, then what about Tom Farber? [In *Foregone Conclusions*] Quantity—100 pages, 98 epigrams, longest 53 words, shortest 4. Quality, phenomenal. Reading, re-reading, ruminating—richly rewarding, no conclusions foregone or forgone.

—Gavan Daws, *Follow The Music*

Thomas Farber has a weird and wonderful mind. He sees everything we see but more. Because he sees more and is so good at saying less, his epigrams translate human experience into playful gems of meaning.

—Leonard Pitt, *Walks Through Lost Paris*

To blurb an epigrammist? Farber—whose wit deserves a whole page—does it himself: "Writer: Someone who can't go without saying."

—Terese Svoboda, *Black Glasses Like Clark Kent's*

Satiric, witty, sarcastic, laconic, Farber's epigrams poke fun at himself, old age, hypocrisy, envy, masturbation, trust funds, hypochondria, support groups, obesity, misanthropy, George W. Bush, pornography, monogamy, poets, suicide, pedophilia, misers, writers, love… His sensitivity to contradiction and paradox, together with his absolute economy and coherence, engaged this reader's wits...

—Zara Raab, *The Book of Gretel*

Thomas Farber, modern master of this ancient form of terse dialectics, has marshalled another collection of gems. Polychromatic, impure. More agate than diamond.

—Iain Boal, *Resisting the Virtual Life*

Tom Farber's *Truth Be Told* offers the sort of wicked pleasures to be found in Gustave Flaubert's *A Dictionary of Platitudes*; here the great fun is (un)leavened by some equally engaging, astute critical prose on the subject of the text: epigrams. The end.

—Binnie Kirshenbaum, *An Almost Perfect Moment*

With pungent wit and cynical insight worthy of Diogenes, Farber's epigrams cast a cold eye on contemporary manners, morals and mortality. His gimlet observations spare no one, least of all their author. A painfully accomplished performance.

—Stephen Kessler, *After Modigliani*

Koans for Cohens
Like *Tones for Joan's Bones*
Too hip for the room

—Ben Sidran, *A Life in the Music*

THE END OF MY WITS

New & Collected Epigrammatics & Companion Essays

Thomas Farber

ANDREA YOUNG ARTS / EL LEÓN LITERARY ARTS
A DEUX FRÈRES BOOK
BERKELEY, CALIFORNIA

The End of My Wits is published by
Andrea Young Arts / El León Literary Arts
A Deux Frères Book

www.andreayoungarts.com
www.elleonliteraryarts.org

Cover and Book Design: Andrea Young

For sales information contact:
Small Press Distribution, Inc.
1341 Seventh Street
Berkeley, CA 94710
www.spdbooks.org

ISBN 978-0-9833919-7-5
LIBRARY OF CONGRESS CATALOG NUMBER: 2012950673

PRINTED IN USA

By Thomas Farber:

FICTION

The Beholder
A Lover's Question
Learning to Love It
Curves of Pursuit
Hazards to the Human Heart
Who Wrote the Book of Love?

NONFICTION

*Akule (*with Wayne Levin*)*
A Lover's Quarrel
*Other Oceans (*with Wayne Levin*)*
*Provocations (*with Robert Kuszek*)*
The Face of the Deep
*Through a Liquid Mirror (*with Wayne Levin*)*
On Water
Compared to What?
Too Soon to Tell
*Rag Theatre (*with Nacio Brown*)*
Tales for the Son of My Unborn Child

EPIGRAMS

The End of My Wits
Foregone Conclusions
Hesitation Marks
The Twoness of Oneness
Truth Be Told
Compressions: A Second Helping
The Price of the Ride

SCREENPLAY

The Two-Body Problem (with Edward Frenkel)

AUTHOR'S NOTE:

Grateful acknowledgement to publishers Donald S. Ellis (*The Price of the Ride*); Peter B. Howard (*Compressions:* A Second Helping); Charles & Gail Entrekin (*Truth Be Told*); and Andrea Young (*The Twoness of Oneness*; *Hesitation Marks*; *Foregone Conclusions*). With minor edits, these chapbooks and books are included here, as well as recent epigrammatics and an extended introduction.

T.F.

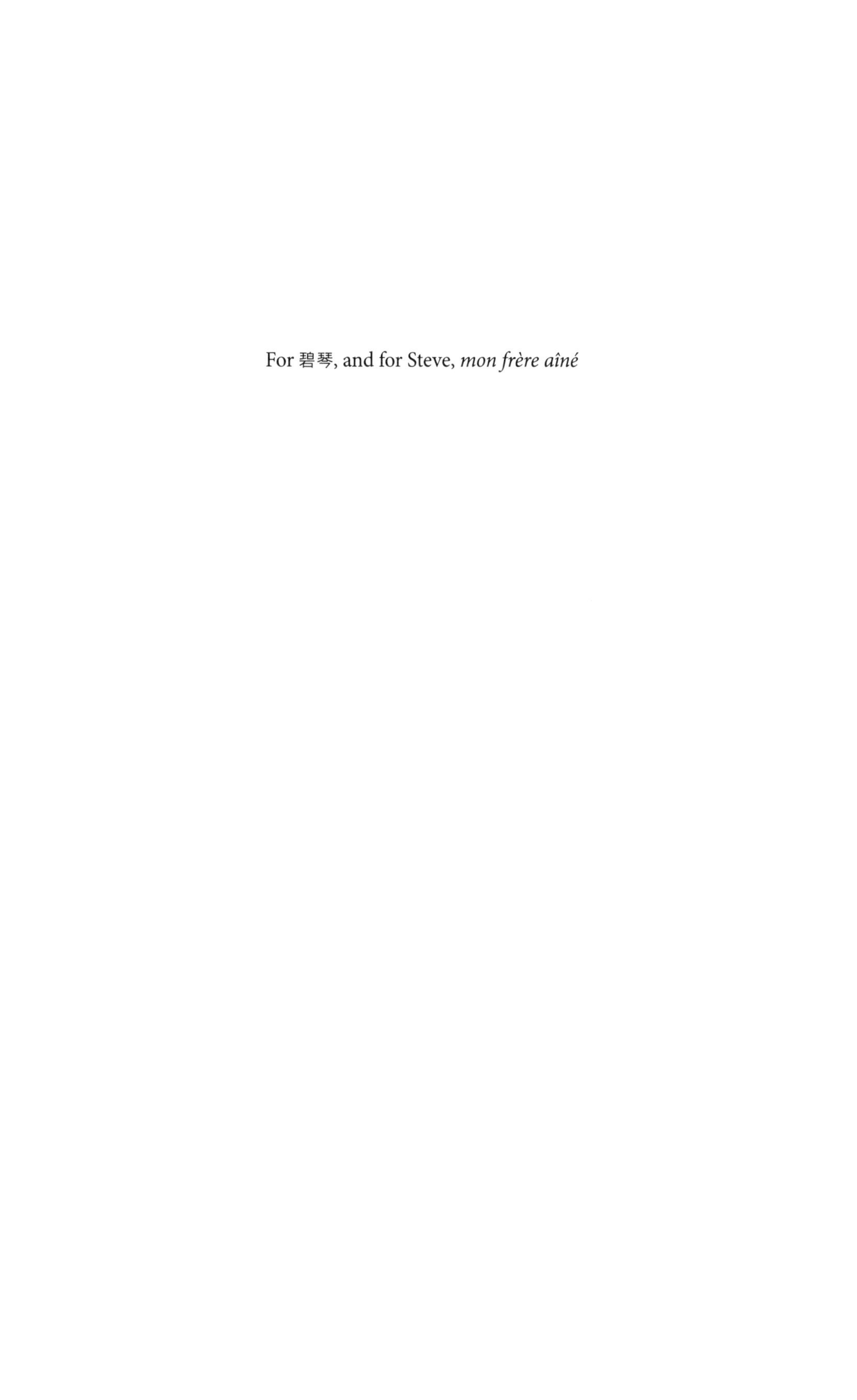

For 碧琴, and for Steve, *mon frère aîné*

CONTENTS:

WHERE WAS I?

And how did it all begin?

The truth will out. In 1993, completing *On Water*, nonfiction about the Pacific, I was abducted by seventeenth century writer Francois (Duc de) La Rochefoucauld. Brutally subjected to his *Maxims*, I found myself...trying some of my own. As it turns out, the ensuing twenty years, among other projects I completed another book of nonfiction about the Pacific, collaborated three times with marine photographer Wayne Levin, dreamed and completed a novel, wrote a memoir, coauthored a screenplay. If the epigrammatic was never all I was up to with language these two decades, neither was it far from my mind, was a kind of default setting. I'd read aphorists; suddenly hear an idiom as if for the first time; tease out component energies of vices, virtues, fallibilities—the compromises we suffer to live with ourselves and others; precise the genesis of this gag reflex, that. Would once more go to my late mother's dictionary to ascertain root, vector. I treasured revelations provoked by unexpected similarities, rejuvenating word inversions, seemingly capricious juxtapositions, willfully mixed metaphors. Here, often as not, to connect the dots—to unpack meaning—the reader would have to be alert, rethink or reread a line that had seemed to require only an instant. Retrace, re-experience(!), the writer's creative process. Further, both form and content were often polemical (Greek, *polemos*, war). Disputatious, controverting. Contentious. And not, of course, just in response to human foible or fate. Also because, even pretending to render the impersonal universal, the implacably authoritative, the writer was (willy-nilly) exposing himself.

In chemistry, sublime's a transitive verb—under extreme pressure, states are changed, impurities left behind. As for human (al)chemistry, in the mid-twentieth century, when I was young, sublimation, like repression, was a defense mechanism you couldn't Freudian-slip your way out of. As the analytic argument went, sublimation's displacement of erotic or aggressive energy into the safe and socially useful (the unacceptable, unwittingly transformed) could only partially satisfy. *Sublimare*, from the Latin, to elevate. Higher, nobler. But dogmas change, paradigms shift; evolutionary biologists ascend. Vocalizations now a primary impulse, perhaps even "pure" play.

This longish compilation of the short, two chapbooks and four small books twenty years in the subliming. Toughened, tempered—annealed!—both by excess and revision's compression. Grist, writer grinding. Procrustean exaggerations, reductions.

Aganactesis: figure of speech in which indignation leads to exclamation. Incisions, correctives, cures. Oddments. Delaminations. Dreads. Excarnations. Micro-fabliaux. Disilluisions. Illluminations. Scourges, wrys. Overexposures. De-obnubilations. Splenetics. Excoriations. Wonderments. Imprecations. Maledictions. Unmaskings. Devilments. All here with companion essays as counterpoint, contrapunt, appraising my fascination with this self-conscious, intemperate form. The accumulation, occasionally, advancing the writer toward *desengano*, state of bittersweet disenchantment.

FBI sketch of the sublimationist, age forty-nine to close to seventy? For a composite, read page by page. As for the malefactor's self-image, think of him as…
—As the boy he was, bantering, bantering with his polylingual brother.
—As one of Napoleon Chagnon's Brazilian Yanomamos: "burly, naked, filthy, hideous..."
—As reader becoming the book in Wallace Stevens' *The House Was Quiet…*
—As Albrecht Durer's fixated draughtsman rapaciously—visually—ingesting a nude.

—As fallen apple fairly close to the family tree, not-quite-spitting image of anatomist-progenitors. Pathologist-father. And mother-poet, who wrote:

> To test a wedding cake:
> use a straw—
> as for a camel's back.

And also:

> Love can be still, and still be love.

In one of what Donald Fanger terms Maxim Gorky's "jottings," Gorky wrote of days everything seemed disgusting—"flowers, chairs, people, the sun," and, of course, himself. "If I am clever enough to live a few more years," Gorky noted, "a very lonely and difficult old age will sneak up on me."

There's a Simon & Garfunkel line, "Hello darkness my old friend." Sometimes, to start writing is to again blindly feel your way in the strangely familiar unknown. Despite the sensation of risk, recurrence has a seductive eros: in darkness you're free to mislead yourself. This while inducing or inflicting a shock of recognition on the reader. Imposing extrapolations, (over) indulging paradoxicality. For French philosophe Jean Beaudrillard, an aphorism was "like the starry sky, the blanks in it being the intersidereral void..." As if anticipating Beaudrillard, Arthur Schnitzler, auteur of his own "thoughts and sayings," wrote, "Shake an aphorism—a lie falls out and a banality remains." Aphorist/poet Don Paterson, well aware he's having his cake and eating it, teases, "A poem is a form of words that advertises its own significance; no more, no less. So with the aphorism, the difference being that all that exists of it is the advertisement."

Ethiopian girl, sixteen, at the nearby high school track. Superb runner. Of course she has no apparent need of the epigrammatic. May it be ever thus.

Still, still...to proffer unsettling analogies; to provoke second thoughts; to magisterially allege the incontrovertibly self-evident; to play the verbal lapidary...Or to chasten, inflicting suffering in the service of moral improvement, not so far from chastising's corporal punishments. All to refine, purify: sometimes the bitter tastes sweet...Or to invoke John of

Gaunt's "tongues of dying men," enforcing "attention like deep harmony."

Prayers for relief: in civil procedure, plaintiff saying what remedies are sought. *Ad quod damnum*, appropriate to the harm. But of course there are limits. And who'd have guessed it would be two decades in the doing, an emerging aggregate with unanticipated properties? Side effects; unintended consequences. Who knew?

Nonetheless, now, surveying these collected forays and mayhems, with retrospect's clarity I confess to having over-savored partiality and the partial. Which is to say: enough blood-letting—the patient died. Enough time in one's version of Proust's cork-lined bedroom, though surely there are worse places. "Gonna' lay down my sword and shield..." Which is to say, let me retract each and every word.

T.F. Berkeley, 2013

I

TRUTH BE TOLD
New & Collected Premortems

(1993-2005, containing *The Price of the Ride*; *Compressions*: A Second Helping; and *Tongue-Tied*: A Breviary of Cautions and Savors, each with companion essay.)

THE PRICE OF THE RIDE (1996)

A man in middle age sitting in an outdoor cafe.
Two young women passing his table,
walking faster than he thinks he'd be able to run after them.

Turning fifty. Avoiding one's older friends.
Lest what's happened to them prove contagious.

The vanity of self-loathing.
He could be deemed a monster, but only by himself.

Sex:
what puts you in contact with people you might otherwise never know.

He took the path of least regret.

Loss of will.
And, also,
loss of won't.

Sir Isaac Newton's gravity: what anyone of a certain age could have explained to him.

“Referred pain”: inappropriate to a particular location, that is to say.

"I love you," she told him. And then, seeing his expression, added, laughing, "But don't worry, I'm very good at unrequited love."

Recently separated. In bed with her lover, she says, "I do things for you I never did for my husband."

Hair on torso, foliating, thickening.
Just when he'd begun to feel really deciduous.

Approaching the end: when a friend thinks of making you both executor and beneficiary of his estate. And, moved to tears, tells you. A kind of trading on the futures exchange.

Fastidious at fifty-five: no inconvenience too small to be avoided.

Not selfish, he was making the world safer for people like himself.

The complex, surprising lives of others. Envy as failure of the imagination.

False modesty: the writer enraged Toni Morrison's won a Nobel Prize, but unable to come up with the name of the someone he'd prefer.

Material times: the going rate of self-interest.

"The only things men fight over are sex and money,"
said the rich womanizer.

To harden one's heart—against God, they used to say.
An idiom now compromised by our understanding of triglycerides.

Remarriage: leads to remodeling.

Remodeling: what precedes a wife's affair with the carpenter.

Apropos of Freud's thesis that a couple always has in the marital bed each mate's parents...Throughout the waning years of his marriage, he often felt the presence of his wife's next husband.

My accountant's wife: after 20 years of marriage, she's left her husband and young daughter for another woman. Years ago, this might have provoked controversy in my circle. Now, it fails even to raise a (pierced) eyebrow.

My accountant's wife, #2: she's come to believe she was a Native American in a previous life. Before the white man's smallpox, she means.

Not his fault: an autodidact, he had a bad teacher.

After careful examination, his self-absorption was found to result not from parental abuse but from a kind of birth defect.

"Gift of tongues." A soul en route to glossolalia but lingering at cunnilingus.

It was the curse of his weak constitution, his greatest health problem, that he could not abide hearing about the maladies of others.

Habitual—preemptive—self-reproach.

He'd grown afraid of winter.

His problem: his soul looks like his body.

There came a point he realized he'd be changed not by traveling but by coming home.

A writer: someone willing to hurt others.

Giacomo Leopardi, 19th century Italian poet, child genius, congenitally deformed, unlucky in love and cursed with poor health. He wrote, "We have seen how very few people will be able to appreciate you when you succeed in becoming a perfect writer."

Very positive fellow. Seeing a therapist at his wife's urging, he learns he suffers from scoptophobia, fear of seeing what's right in front of one's eyes.

Speaking as a failed vegetarian...

Paolo Uccello, 15th century Florentine painter who established the rules of linear perspective. As Vasari wrote, "To pore over these things he remained in seclusion for months at a time," which apparently kept him impoverished. According to Uccello's wife, Uccello would work all night, and when she asked him to rest, he'd reply, "Oh, what a delightful thing is this perspective."

AFTERWORD

1993. I was forty-nine—me, once always the youngest, now going on fifty?—and *On Water* was soon to be published. I'd been saved by writing about water, by spending so much time in and on it the previous ten years. Doing so, having to do so, despite the risk that too much might be washed away. But then, suddenly, I was obsessed with—incessantly reading, and eager to learn the craft of, the import of—epigrams, aphorisms, apothegms. Nietzsche, Leopardi, Joubert, Chamfort, La Rochefoucauld, Lichtenberg, Porchia, Kraus, Jabès, Connolly, Martial, Pascal, Wilde, Chazal, Valery, Cioran, Cunningham, Canetti. It might have been a cleansing of the writer's palate, but if I'd once been drawn to prose out of an impulse for the comprehensive, for narrative, now I wanted my stories very short, if stories at all.

Of course writing's a form of argument, an attempt to convince the reader that one character or another deserves sympathy, that this is how the world works, is the language of understanding. But as I got into the epigrammatic, I was interested most in the argument's conclusion. The story a given, or excluded except as backdrop. The form's very brevity an argument: why labor the obvious? As for the sentiments expressed... Well, my mood was wintry, an insistence on the human capacity for self-deception in the service of self-interest. And my language—oh, compressed, requiring attention, perhaps even a dictionary at hand.

But did I say argument? All this was peculiarly one-sided, left the reader little room for dialogue with the author, was almost pure assertion. Each short piece seemed to imply an unstated *quod erat demonstrandum*. Q.E.D.

Kronenberger, in his introduction to Merwin's translation of Chamfort, writes:

> English is a natural language for the aphorism. Unlike French, English can dispense with both the definite and indefinite article, can let the genitive ride on the nominative's back, and prepositions dance at sentences' ends; and can thus be more pointed, more concise, more splendidly lapidary.

And it's true, for writer as craftsman there is an enormous delight in working this form. But content and tone are something else. Martial, in the first century A.D., and then La Rochefoucauld, in the seventeenth century, seem to have defined the form's air of disenchantment, the voice of the fallen or banished aristocrat. The men's hut, male writers in middle age. As Joseph Epstein writes, "The bone truth is that aphorisms, while they need not be bitter, are usually better for being so." And as La Bruyere argued, "No vice exists which does not pretend to be more or less like some virtue, and which does not take advantage of this assumed resemblance."

There was on the other hand the wistful Antonio Porchia, a real seeker: "Sometimes at night I light a lamp so as not to see." Of Porchia's epigrams, Merwin wrote, "The distillate of suffering in some of the entries is pure and profound irony," but though I admired Porchia, he wasn't what I was after. Perhaps because, as Merwin observed, Porchia's was "an irony not of defense but of acceptance." No, I preferred, say, Lichtenberg, found overstatement well worth the risk: "A book is a mirror—when a monkey looks in, no apostle looks back out."

Martial and La Rochefoucauld. Playfully cruel. Acid. Scabrous: rough, harsh, somewhat indelicate. Passionate but detached, as if without illusions. Moralists moralizing. Punishing, implicating the reader with hard truths, forcing agreement. Self-absorbed, risking self-pity.

If the blues are an American idiom, in part because their formulaic laments are so confessional (Oprah Winfrey inevitably follows), epigrams are un-American. We believe in second chances, in mobility, insist we're a classless society. Our own most native epigrammatic impulse comes in the tag lines of Country and Western songs—"If the phone doesn't ring it's just me;" or "She got the gold mine, I got the shaft." Amiable, wry, and clever, but, as with the Porchia, not what I was after.

The darker aspect of words. As revenge, for example: Swiftian, the adjective. Which means? Well, Swift's Gulliver, back home from his travels, unable to abide the stench of humans. Avoiding wife and children by staying out in the stable with the horses, who remind him of Houyhnhnmland's four-legged creatures of true reason. Misanthropy: hatred, distrust, of the species. The triumph of honesty over hope, some say. Thackery: "Ah, Vanitas Vanitatum! Which of us is happy in this world? Which of us has his desire? Or, having it, is satisfied?— Come, children, let us shut up the box and the puppets, for our play is played out."

As I worked in and around this form, I'd phone friends to convey what I was up to. They'd laugh, ruefully, thought what they heard trenchant, tough. But later, several readers of the manuscript deemed my brevities, collectively, bleak, merciless, mean. Mean-spirited. Which left me disappointed, not in the news but in my friends. That is, I felt they were having trouble facing the truth. A bit late in the day, it seemed to me, for Pangloss, or to be getting squeamish.

Another friend, a very goodhearted poet (more positive a soul than I, but also old enough to know that one has to work at being goodhearted), observed that epigrams could lead right into silence. "At the end of that road is silence," is how she put it. And this, I had to admit, had merit. It wasn't simply that many of my compressions had to do with dying/death or foible/folly, but that they were, finally, a screed against language, against even bothering to continue the conversation. Which seemed to me at least one appropriate response to the world as I was experiencing it, like the behavior of the tribe that ceases to have children when its population falls below a certain level. Things were getting weird, no? When my sweet-souled poet friend, in any case, said that such epigrams could lead to silence, I responded, "There are worse things than silence."

If, however, I believed my epigrammatic writing had good cause, never did I not know that this was dabbling in a kind of black magic. Not just the adolescent's bad behavior, or not even the coke freak's high, achieved with the understanding that the moment will be brief, the coming down rocky, the insights neon.

Perhaps all art's black magic—Prospero's wand. No policemen in the heart and soul of the artist, as Conrad observed. Often, cackling madly after hammering out yet another line, I'd think of a friend in southern California who'd become a compulsive writer of letters-to-the-editor. Long since, his brilliant calumnies had little to do with any effort to change minds.

About a year after I first noticed I'd become obsessed with the epigrammatic, I received a fellowship for a trip to Samoa: fallout from the water book. As I turned my attention to gathering materials for this return to the South Pacific, I noticed my addictive delight in the epigrammatic beginning to moderate, though I did start culling what I'd come up with, preparing a short 'final' manuscript. A writer is someone who finishes things...But the relentless need I'd had to write my compressions, as if they contained a mineral without which I could not survive, had abated. There is a tradition of eating dirt, in both Africa and in the American South. Geophagy: hungering for a certain taste or sustenance to the point of eating soil. "The practice is found among peoples of low culture throughout the world," says the outdated *Webster's New International*, Second Edition, "and often develops an appetite or craving which favors idiocy...etc." Not that I'd finished with the form—there was so much still to learn; I could spend years emulating Martial alone. Exposing myself to him, so to speak. Seeing what he brought out in me. But though I still wanted to pursue the craft of the epigrammatic, the sentiments the form seemed to induce in me no longer cried out to be expressed. And/or, I'd begun to tire of paradox, oxymoron, antithesis. Suddenly, inversions and apparent contradictions were too inevitable. Predictable, for all their surprises.

On my return from Samoa, when I once more made a decision to sit down at my desk, start that kind of travel—no passport needed—it was story, of all things, that was again an imperative. Everything and anything, past and present, what I could remember or reconstruct, what I knew or could imagine of the lives of others, all of it suddenly seemed both accessible and vital to speak of. I began writing at a ferocious pace. And after a month of early winter rain, there came a time when, heading out for my double cappuccino at dawn one November morning, I looked and saw a beautiful crescent cupping and illuminating the globe of the moon, fist of Jupiter pulsing just above. Saw, and wanted—oh, needed—to say so.

(1996)

COMPRESSIONS: A Second Helping (1998)

"You do not know what life you live, or what you do, or who you are."

—Dionysius in Euripides' *Bacchae*

The bells of Hell go ting-a-ling-a-ling
For you but not for me.

—sung by WWI British troops

"I never lie," he says. Through his teeth, as it were.

"I never lie," he says. To others, he means.

Audible silence. The story of her life was she'd resolved not to tell it.

Zen of secrecy's eros: sound of one self-pleasuring.

Promiscuous secrecy.

"You wasted your life," she says, flattering both herself and him.

"Beneath contempt." Down there somewhere.

Gratitude? Sing need, need.

Kissing cousins: opinion, hypocrisy.

Raised voices (should) raise skepticism.

Writer in study: house arrest.

Not, of course, that he'd set out to become an unpublished writer.

That poem? Second-rate prose failing to go the distance.

What people don't see is how much work it was not to hold a job.

He claimed an emotional deduction for the cost of being rich.

Home Ec: on balance, cheaper to love than to hate.

Their marriage worked until the market started to fall.

She loves her husband, whom she deceives with a lover she deceives by letting him believe she loves him.

Said the adulteress to her lover, "You're more interested in my marriage than I am."

"My wife," he frequently says, even to those who know her proper name.

Her apparent hatred of her former husband was really just shame.

One of his palms cupping each breast. “I wish you had a third hand,” she says.

She's lived with her boyfriend five years, never married because he doesn't want to, finally has an affair, is jilted by her lover. Seeing her so unhappy, the boyfriend proposes.

Wilt Chamberlain's "20,000" lovers. Yo, Wilt: Names? Birthdays?

Know thyself: “Good thing I’m powerless,” he muttered.

A Jew who veers Republican should have his foreskin examined.

Sweet sorrow: regret become rue.

Remorse: biting one's own back.

Suicide, indirect indicator of strength: how long he'd been able to put up with himself.

“Don’t speak ill of the dead.”
An enjoinder now attributed to J. Edgar Hoover.

“Don’t speak ill of the dead.”
Next thing you know, they’ll be telling us not to speak ill of the living!

“He deserved to die,” she said. “He got off light.”

FURTHER THOUGHTS ON THE EPIGRAMMATIC

> Evolutionary psychology argues that excessive self-knowledge can be . . .a hindrance. If people perceive you as good and benevolent, they are more likely to accede to your desires. A good way to get others to believe that you are good and benevolent is to believe it yourself. —Oliver Morton

As readers of *The Price of the Ride* have seen, the afterthoughts and repercussions of that short book did not exhaust my interest in brevity, paradox, or foible. Nor did these half-truths requite my desire to encourage the reader to risk the distance from premise to conclusion. As Jesse Green argues, the reader must "work out, and usually backward, what trajectory led from takeoff to landfall…" Though Green believes such a task is created with "more than a hint of sadism," I confess only to be asserting that this is the world we live in, the tongue of understanding. Using the enchantment of language to express…oh, aspects of disenchantment, brief briefs about or against what we profess to hold to be true.

Given my experience in this form, what words come to mind to further describe its component energies ? Well…

TEMPTATION. "I have written a wicked book," Melville wrote Hawthorne about Moby Dick, "and feel spotless as the lamb." Surely, stripping away narrative in favor of conclusion, the epigrammist savors the risk of being wrongheaded/reductionist/unfair.

RETALIATION, though the form may appear to possess a first strike capability. The proverbial revenge against reality. And, always, what one would like to have said. *Avoir un esprit de l'escalier*: one's belated repartee—*quand il n'est plus temps, qui se manifeste en retard*—as, out the door, one heads down the staircase. "I as much as told him," a friend of mine said, recounting an argument he was winning in the retelling.

BONSAI, a mix of envisioning, pruning, shaping, caring. Stunting. Making something perfect, if on a diminished scale. Improving(?) nature. Delight in doing something harder than it looks.

POINTILLISM, going after the luminous by small discrete increments, dots of color the hues of which are to be mixed, recomposed, made into shapes by the reader's eye.

As for the views of others about such endeavor, after reading *The Price of the Ride* a friend claimed a line as his own. Maybe he'd heard me tell it to him before? Nope. Whatever: not my favorite, I explained. Someone else felt a fragment was about him. I did what I could—"It's an if-the-shoe-fits type of deal," I said. And a poet I know observed that epigrams are "poems without wings." This good writer momentarily perhaps not "afraid enough of poetry," as George Oppen put it.

Another correspondent suggested the little book as a whole made a kind of ghazal? *Zhazam*! An ancient form, it turns out— short lyrics, couplets intensely compressed—from Persian literature, appearing later in Urdu poetry, part of the Islamic legacy. But my work a ghazal? Go figure.

Ghazal or no, I had been obsessed with compression. Even early on in my prose experience, what to leave out in story compelled as much as what to put in. I thought mastery more possible within a small frame, an odd notion, perhaps. By the time *Who Wrote the Book of Love?* (1977) was published, I'd been working in prose units no longer than several pages, some of these fables of contemporary life only half a page, none with titles, characters often unnamed.

By *Compared to What?*(1988), my third-person nonfiction meditation on writing and the writer's life, I felt free to have "chapters" one or two lines long. I liked the white space, saw no reason poets should have sole possession of such rich terrain. A "Take Back the Night" situation, as far as I was concerned. Poet/translator Stephen Mitchell, reading an early draft of *The Price of the Ride*, suggested that setting the brevities one or two to a page would test their strength. Right he was, but I also enjoyed the sensation that so much blank page was illicit. (Edmond Jabès believed white space "is much stronger and more violent than the text...It's necessary that writing have a great space in and of itself to support the white space.")

The epigrammatic. Jesse Green writes, "Where pornography is rape, wit must be, too, for wit is intellectual pornography, stimulating for the sake of stimulation..." Here I demur, and not only because pornography is not rape, whatever the delight of so erroneous a comparison. Really, wit's just another kind of pleasure, but, in the epigrammatic, didactic: hard truths are broached, cases made. If we are to consider the epigrammatic and sex, perhaps the link is to foreplay, however penetrating the insight.

Finally, inevitably, the question of misanthropy. Are these premortems, mordents, tarts & tales bad for the spirit? No medicinal value—diuretic, if not cathartic? Surely it's worth something to articulate such complexities as the music of language allows. Then too, there's the joy of trying to achieve the verbal equivalent of a prime number. Of working one's way toward the irreducible and so untranslatable. Forget the even theoretical possibility of paraphrase! What was said, is. And though bitterness may be the risk of satire, we may conclude that love of even the weapon is, nonetheless, a form of love.

To know more than one can say.
Or so say I.
Told you so.
Tell you what.
You know what I mean.

(1998)

TONGUE-TIED: A Breviary of Cautions & Savors (2005)

Breviary: a book of daily prayers, from Latin, *breviarium*, abridgement.

It's hard to be human and hide the wet spot.
—Dr. William Santis

Q: Have I wasted my whole life?

A. No. Not yet.

Spring makes light of winter's sorrows.

He wouldn't recognize the truth if it walked past him naked.

Surprising, not that he lived alone, but that he could live with himself.

Alone. Why people get cats, dogs. Married.

Spacious bedroom. Room for misunderstanding.

Not a turn-on: she'd never been spanked as a child.

She hopes he doesn't fuck like he eats.

Right, humor's aggressive component.
But then, difference between a joke and a war?

He tells her, “You’re my soul.” Which he fails to save.

Yo, jilted lovers! Don’t argue with the dead when they’re still alive.

He died not of heartbreak but from a case of severely strained credulity.

His adultery was the high-minded kind.

Devoted to both wife and lover. Loyal to a fault.

Calmly pointing out the obvious, the Zen acolyte notes that Jesus's violent demise shows He had "unfinished business." An argument perhaps best resolved when the acolyte's on his own deathbed. Or cross.

Q. Since nothing happens without a higher purpose, what was the higher purpose when the spiritual seeker left his wife?
A: To be with another woman.

Writer. Blocked? Or, nothing he's willing to confess.

Writer's block? Like everyone, writers block out quite a bit.

Charity to a friend, then melancholy.
Dismay at the friend's fate?
Self-pity?

Writer, home from a fellowship abroad, informs listeners that travel broadens. William Blake, Emily Dickinson, and Henry David Thoreau having, so to speak, missed the boat.

"Being famous is hard," the writer confides, startling the interviewer, who'd understood her to be momentarily newsworthy.

Selfish writer. Philanthropist of the arts.

Passion's nomenclature. "Whore:" what her lover called her for fucking her husband.

Still with her husband-the-jogger? Cuckolds have legs!

Afraid. Of, for instance, being alone with a book.

Quiet. Worth a great deal.
Too quiet. Worth even less.

Capable of doing without, her sacrifices were mostly human.

The atomic half-life of self-deprecation. Always briefer than the need to deprecate others.

Penis: Clinical, like vulva, most frequently qualified only by the possessive, i.e., his penis. Prick, on the other hand, like cunt, can take another adjective or two.

Concluding she seemed virginal but wasn't, he resolved to privilege not adjectives but nouns.

“Still in love?” the husband offers by way of salutation, before one can ask after his wife the heiress.

"You're larger than life," they tell him. That is:
1. they fear they're not really living, and
2. they're glad not to be larger than life.

Viagra'd penis: friend standing up for you.
Viagra'd penis: mind of its own.
Viagra joke? Penis as standup comedian.
Viagra: makes your member remember.
Rap Viagra: got yo' back? Naw, yo' front.

Using the word small for one's partner's penis? Self-fulfilling; self-denying.

Fans at ball games screaming obscenities.
A kind of Halloween, but is it masks on, or masks off?

Idiomatic American English:
Not very easy: “Please.”
Surprisingly difficult: “You’re welcome.”

Jealousy:
demanding proof of what never happened;
indicted for hyperbole, guilty of understatement;
equals self-knowledge.

Free translation...*Preposterous*, from the Latin. Ass backwards.

You haven't really lived 'til you don't want to live anymore.

"As good as dead." And gettin' better all the time.

Obituaries, death notices.
Death notices?
Sure: Death doesn't miss a living thing.

Winter darkness. The end is nigh(t).

Epitaph:
SEE YOU SOON

Last line of our tale?
Death sentence.

TESTAMENTS & MEA CULPAS

Recently, I turned sixty. Sixty—a wonder-working number as thirty, forty, fifty never were. Over the years, I'd experienced a bemused remove from the dismay of others confronting such benchmarks. But sixty? I felt...fast-forwarded. Victim of mistaken identity. Read the digits as a measure of my debt to time, like a losing gambler at evening's end who'd almost convinced himself the chips were...just chips.

More, I was faintly embarrassed, as if having contracted a social disease. Sixty? Not that there wasn't fair warning. As I turned fifty-four, an artery in my heart tried to "occlude." Close call, but life went on. Then, two years ago, I became the friend of a woman in her mid-thirties who worked with "seniors," the "over-sixties." Of course I realized I'd soon qualify to be one of her clients. Picking her up at work, I couldn't fail to see wheelchairs in the lobby. Wheelchairs are for others? Also, receiving still another fifth-year report from my college class, I was sobered by the growing number of death notices. Memento mori: Remember that thou must die. I'd presumed an exemption. Son of a famous physician who built the world's first hospital for the care of children with cancer—about a mile from our beautiful home—I grew up able to make an absolute distinction between those dying kids and my siblings and self. Years later, arriving in California at twenty, I had the sensation there was no dying here, so much milder the climate, so much freer of the dead hand of the past than my native Boston.

Just sixty, then, and though sixty's the former fifty, I reread "The Snow Man," Wallace Stevens arguing you need "a mind of winter" to behold "the boughs/Of the pine trees crusted with snow." A mind of winter: this time, the phrase spoke both of one's response to the physical world and to my animus for a third batch of very brief winter's tales.

See the dying man? "Not long for this world," they say, albeit—albeit! —less than they used to. "Not long for this world." Passing out of usage. Archaic because of the hint of euphemism, suggestion of something to come? When, recently, I heard the phrase uttered by a vital eighty-four year old doctor/surfer in Honolulu, the words entered my ears as imperative: you should not long for this world. Though of course we do, we do.

Composing oneself. The last four decades (ha!, the erotics of being able to invoke so much misspent time)...I say, the last four decades I've been impelled to write from a not unusual mix of motives. Emulating books I admired; sense of author as hero, magician; exhilaration of supplicating, dancing with, language. Hunger to set straight, restore. Not to mention words like vainglory, memorialize, lament. But as the writer ages, whatever his habitual mode or fluency, though the number of letters in the alphabet remains constant, stories written and unwritten seem to undergo transformation. At the least, by a certain age the author surely better knows of what he speaks. Can sometimes more freely acknowledge self-interest, self-deception. Concede the limits of art: how much can it redeem; for whom redemptive?

Alternatively, p.o.v. of the text, perhaps stories increasingly manifest their own agenda. "Yo, this is your story speaking." Might the stories be compared to:

1. teenage males, voices cracking, tremulously insisting on their own (passionately contrary) narrative of what you thought you'd been living with them?

2. caged lions that, after years of compliance, maul the tamer?

3. terrorist sleeper cell biding its time?

Or perhaps there are different storytelling centers within each of us.

Imagine Freud's imaginary Ego, Superego, and Id each having its own narrative. Imagine three or five other aspects of the self! Perhaps all their stories are always being told, like radio stations sending out signals at the same time, but as years pass the writer has less strength to insist on "his" version. To resist the stories' version? For the male writer, it may coincide with the waning of testosterone haze, occasioning a new—pristine; bewildering—ability, willingness, to see. Or perhaps stories never do not know they're only stories, and—approaching our end, which is to say, their host's demise—note that our blood is thinning, are not reluctant to let on.

But how plumb the motives of stories? Perhaps, instead, we should think in terms of the visual—a mere change of perspective. For years, it's all mostly before you; room for improvement, correction. The triumph of Your Real Story can still take place, to which the past is subordinated. But what's behind you accumulates; space for new narrative foreshortens, unless you're extending your saga into The Life to Come, which has its own hazards—Hell, for instance…

There may even be some concomitant enlightenment. Think of the heroic polar explorer stranded on the ice floe who, eating his shoe, finally acknowledges no rescue's forthcoming. A coming to terms perhaps influenced by the sight of shoe-eating colleagues. No rescue. Why, then, do some—most?—writers persist in their earlier narratives? Oh, adult life as nursery school, cont'd: one more gold star on the forehead. Why be reckless in service of the truth, what if you can beat the game, if there's no reckoning? What if the disguise still works, or truth's just too painful. For writer, audience. Lear terrifies, but, leaving the theatre, we reestablish distance: foolish Lear, and a king to boot! Not like us, and we have no heaths over here anyway. But those gold stars on the forehead. Think of poets playing the poet. What if each oracular pronunciamento takes one further from what he might have been able to say? "Poetry as breath," for instance. Oh, Jeez, kiss my breath. So many fairytales about our lives, told by writers.

Q: So, T.F., your "cautions and savors" tell the whole truth?

A: Nope. Sorry. Epigrams are, well, polished shards. Karl Kraus said "an aphorism never coincides with the truth," is "either a half-truth or a one-and-a-half truth." Whether or not that is true, epigrams may be breadcrumbs marking the writer's path home to...silence, or to more extended prose. Or may function as prods, reminding the word-worker about word joy. Or implicate, soberingly, once more evoking the personal the writer projected as universal, what Kafka called transforming I-madness into he-madness.

For the American writer, another appeal of the epigrammatic is its near—utter—unmarketability. What *is* the relationship of writer and audience? Disdain (dis+deign)? Perhaps too strong a word, and often paired with craven need, but how little response should one hope for? Years ago, working as a consultant at a foundation-funded conference, well-paying labor in a good cause, I sat in a hotel banquet room suffering through interminable first-day Power-Pointed remarks. Sand rivering down, down through the waist of life's hourglass. Looking over at my colleague's laptop as he typed frenetically—conference journaling, I thought; hard working to a fault—I realized my colleague was completing an overdue report for another foundation. Our eyes met. "Fuck 'em if they can't take a joke," he said. Kept typing. Though, soon after the conference, my colleague died prematurely—alcohol; cigarettes; angry wit—I now, as epigrammist, often think of his admonition.

But my manuscript. Only lately, *Tongue-Tied* was still awaiting 'completion.' I'd been working at it four years, now and then coming up with another one-liner. Revising the accumulation yet again, trying to get at core verbal impulse. For several months, however, I'd done little 'real' writing. Mostly teaching, salsa dancing, a commissioned film treatment, email. I liked being in the 'pure present tense,' as I construed it, how I imagine most people live, though I did miss the closure of my study, routine of solo labor, all that order to keep. Not 'really' writing, in any case, I'd reached the point I could no longer tell whether I was doing myself a favor or inflicting deprivation. Avoiding or inducing megalomania.

Meanwhile, in Hawai'i—surfing, more salsa—I set myself the task of rereading my recent novel, *The Beholder* (2001). Took four weeks to get through it, assessing words, sentences, structure of scenes, remembering what was left out, reworked how through so many drafts. DVD of my novel, with Bonus Features! Was, in the end, moved, admiring. Not self-congratulatory: another self wrote it, in another lifetime—five years earlier for the first draft, and that initial applied dreaming built on years of reading and research (!) about pornography and representations of the nude female form. (Around the time I'd turned sixty, an old friend came across *The Beholder*, called to say she loved it. "You must have women lined up at the front door waiting to seduce the author." I put down the phone, went to check.)

So: back from Hawai'i, I began to edit the interview Melville scholar Sam Otter had conducted with me about my Pacific writings, in particular my many references to *Moby Dick*. At one point I'd said to Sam, "There I was in the Pacific. I needed it. I had the great feeling almost nobody else was writing about this world with candor, much less with skill...I felt I owned it." Reading these lines, I was suddenly impelled to again think of myself as a writer, as if I'd remembered a terribly important appointment at the last possible moment. An "Ah, of course" sort of deal. And at this moment, what kind of writer would I be? There by my desk was the folder of unpublished epigrams, one to a page, pulsing on the shelf like my computer's green light in "Sleep" mode. I'd been letting them...mature, stew, metastasize. Manifest their weaknesses. In that instant of recovery of the writerly self, or of once more displacing some better self, I was again an epigrammist, member of a small, strange cohort, but once more entitled to its malices, savors, ripostes, errors. At this moment, the labor was hands-on, shaping, smoothing. Wordsmith as bikini wax specialist crafting the perfect Brazilian cut. "Far out," as they used to say in the days I had long hair. I was, happily, back at work.

And in my orbit, as always, other artists at work. Young Michael, teaching himself to be a writer, reading my books carefully, gleaning. Very talented Laura, year five on her novel. Leo, eighty, with the manuscript of a masterful new story collection. Chester, past eighty, still centering his passionate life around the freedom to write, publishing one new book, another. Also in my orbit, as always, artists not at work: H, for instance, who has the latest computer and ergonomic chair but is unable to sit still at his desk. Where did that capacity go? Perhaps for too long he didn't risk enough, in the end forgot how. Committing to words is a tough game.

Committing to words. Joyce Carol Oates, in *The Faith of a Writer*, argues: "To write is to invite angry censure...Art by its nature is a transgressive act, and artists must accept being punished for it. The more original and unsettling their art, the more devastating their punishment."

Q: Tom, what do you think of that quote?

T.F: Must I answer?

Q: Please.

T.F. Well...yes, no. Sometimes. Actually, the more common curse of art is that you may not be sure you deserve praise. Or, one's own judgments may be the most severe. Lately, for instance, I've been subjected to a nightly predawn barrage of berating, and not from others. Surely this too will pass. In addition, I've found myself easily moved to tears. Just the kind of thing my mother would have deplored. And bad for the epigrammist? Well, there's Frost's line, "No tears in the writer, no tears in the reader." But I also think of my friends in Boston so many, many years ago, how among ourselves we ten-year-olds talked tough and surly. Eat it raw; old enough to bleed/old enough to butcher; up yours; no shit, Dick Tracy. Add a few other lines, and you'd achieve fluency in our lingua franca. But we also well knew what it was to be "crying mad," to turn away from the sight of tears in others. For the grownup epigrammist, then, perhaps the motto should be "No flinching." Something we kids used to say, in moments long ago long lost, when it was again our turn to strike the blow.

(2005)

II

THE TWONESS OF ONENESS:

Apologues, Ripostes & (Dis)Enchantments (2008)

Old man, difficult, complaining, dying. Unbecoming.

The man who could do almost anything for himself, being French-kissed.

Young woman. Making out, but not consummating.
Near Miss.

Some night the sun will die.
Death, too.

Out there somewhere, one's late parents, death-mutes listening to words we say were theirs.

Promises, comparative price check: not kept v. not made.

Habitually late—and resolved not to die young.

Envisioning previous lovers, in her.
Oneself, retrospectively, odd man out.

Apprehending one's lover, but failing to mention the right to remain silent.

Swami Muktananda said, "The only thing you lose when you die is your fear of death." When you encounter Swami in the Great Hereafter, take a moment to be sure he has all his fingers and toes.

Evidence of life after death? Overruled: insubstantial; immaterial.

Old age. Farewells-in-progress, some not articulated.
Oneself in the mirror: person to whom you must be sure to say goodbye.

Lecher (from the French, to lick): a man "immoderately given to sexual indulgence" as characterized by the immoderately envious.

Sincerely confessional poet, seventy-five. Ever-affable lip still buttoned about insider award trading, or about giving the wife, beloved dedicatee, venereal microbes bestowed by one muse or another. The confessional poet does, however, publish a New and Selected Poems with a villanelle about passing gas, five tercets and closing quatrain of smoke blown up the reader's netherend. Grave pending, it's all asses to asses.

Network of poets: cronyism, unsung.

Shocked by lipstick on his collar, yet loath to be convinced. But oh, that fragrance. Smelling is (dis)believing.

His was the anger of those who feel entitled to understand.

The "sort of boyfriend" of the woman I started sleeping with.
Farther along we got, farther along they got.

Bush & Cheney, itching for war with Iran. Long lost, the youthful courage of their Vietnam-era lack of conviction.

Bush & Cheney: to admit torture would cause discomfort.

Narcissists, envied: too lucky in love.

At the buffet table of sexual pleasure, the masturbatrix helped herself.

So many people standing around, waiting to die. Suicides as control freaks.

Age thirty-one, he conveyed the impression he could always go home and live with his parents.

Marriage vow v. courtroom oath: nothin’ ’bout “nothing but the truth.”

“Who gives a shit?” the asshole asked, neglecting to wipe his mouth.

"I might..."
Maysayer.

One-night stand, interrupted during sex, while in the middle of something or Other.

Limbs intertwined, eyes glazed: orgasm achieved, the amnesiacs are unable to recall who/what/where/when. Or why.

Hypocrites (from the Greek—actor, pretender). Generally, takes one to know one.

Failures of the imagination: envy; some kinds of lying.

Expert at laying out an argument though not so good at questioning premises, he sees clearly what may not be so.

Cuba in the 1950s. Batista's brutal dictatorship,
miraculous Afro-Cuban polyrhythms.
Like Che, young Fidel just could not dance:
two left feet.

Humans resist emotional exposure, protect aspects of privacy. Feign, affect, seem. As for pretenses, how can they be anything but false?

Turning seventy, her fifth wedding day. Old School, she's never had a lover she didn't marry, but this time around she'll be faithful 'til the grave.

Promiscuous. Too many partners? Or just plain single-minded.

Talking to oneself too much: not spoken for.

Sidewalk, old man pretends to need directions from teenager, tells her how beautiful she is, asks where she goes to school. Her reluctance to seem rude now mixed with unease. His pleasure in this? Bending the girl to his will, she not knowing what he'd do if he could just bend her over, if he could still bend over.

Lived alone. For want of a better alternative.

Lived alone. For not-want of a better alternative.

Successful and rich, the Dartmouth grad's still rankled by not being admitted to Harvard decades ago. Though Harvard, deplorably, did have a quota for Jews, that year it accepted several of his Jewish high school classmates. Perhaps, then, Harvard had a second quota, for young men kind of like him.

Rich and beautiful, forestalling envy she denigrated herself. Envied the enviers.

Prepuce: fold of skin covering the tip of the penis or, homologically, the clitoris. If, like some others, you deplore circumcision, consider Christ's Foreskin, only thing here on earth He left behind. A holy relic the Catholic faithful deem responsible for countless miraculous pregnancies.

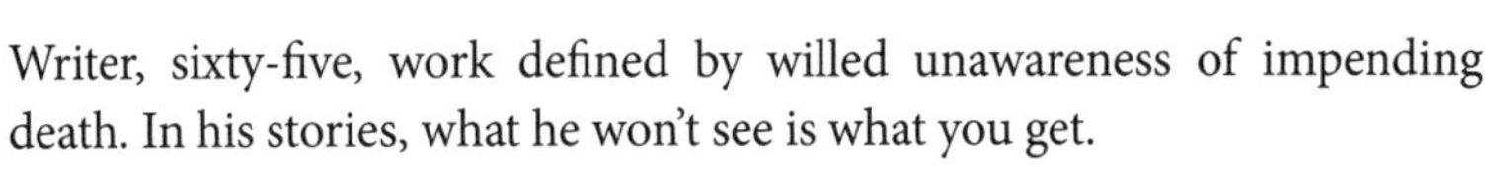

Writer, sixty-five, work defined by willed unawareness of impending death. In his stories, what he won't see is what you get.

Famous author, eighty, bullish on the future, discussing work-in-progress with ambitious young writers. As if he and they are on the same page.

American English circa 1959: ‘getting in her pants’ generally preceded by ‘I love you.’

For the time being. Humans as timed beings.

One of "the people" in the 1960s, now, driving a new Mercedes-Benz SUV, he has both collision insurance and an expression arguing "functional; richly deserved."

Married a year now, he's put on weight.

Posthumous fame—good?
Or, already envying your name for outliving you.

Poor unenviable envy, sometimes not much worse than strong need defending itself.

Sixty-four. Life expectancy, eighty-one and a half.
Seventeen years. Time metronoming, "where-ya-goin', where-ya-goin'?"

Sixty-four. Life expectancy, eighty-one and a half.
Seventeen years. When he started college, seventeen was all he knew.

Not so as anyone could really tell, but she hated herself for being hateful.

S's. Refuse, verb. Refuse, noun.

Dirt=d'earth? Nope: from Scandinavian, drit=shit.

Noun, adjective. Hard 'c,' soft 'c.' Rancor, rancid.

No free lunch for the well off. To pick up or not pick up the group's dinner tab; to get, or keep, a job; explaining there'll have to be a pre-nup; how, not starving, to play the artist; or, being really comfortable only with one's own kind.

Males in post–de Tocqueville America—any man a king!—admit to envy, but not to feeling inferior.

The other side of the story. But, getting there from here?

The dead of night. Who are...

“Pornography is rape”—1980s argument with a certain thrust to it. Hyperbole as verbal violence, forcing submission to the arguers’ (rapacious) fantasy of dominating the private lives of others.

Drowning in the sea of love. Not flotsam: jetsam.

The Spanish conquistadors slaughtered the Indians of the Caribbean for being "sodomites." Opposites attract.

Secretive writer. Soon-to-be-published novel the only thing forthcoming about him.

Though fiction's lying, the writer thought crafting it would make an honest man of him.

Heaven: sop invented by the living to appease the dead.

Heaven: sop for the poor invented by the rich, subsequently also a sop for some of the rich.

Some life forms never have sex, die, they say, only from external hazards. Life forms that do have sex always die.

Naïve greed: as if things can be improved!

His pained look? Trying to decide whether to conceal what he thought or pretend to think otherwise.

Freud argued hate's older than love, which could mean it'll die first.

The dead: invisible but not inaudible.

Writer: someone who can’t go without saying.

WHAT MADE HIM DO IT AGAIN?

> Dirt, then, is never a unique, isolated event.
> Where there is dirt there is system.
> —Mary Douglas, *Purity and Danger*

All's well that ends well. A good time was had by all. Happily ever after.

Age 63, the writer's back from Paris; French rights to his novel *The Beholder* have been sold; and he's completed a final draft of a second memoir, *Brief Nudity*. Meanwhile, young 碧琴 has entered his life, suddenly in residence. Unexpected miracle. Though he'd thought he'd be traveling—Thailand; New York City—they're staying close to home. Making room for her in the cottage and the garage/library after years of living alone, he starts culling books, setting box after box out on the curb, watching footprints of his path as a writer vanish. In the process, he encounters once again his library's sex and death alphabets and adjoining shelves of the epigrammatic or books unveiling aspects of character. Malcolm de Chazal, Harold Brodkey, Machiavelli, Pauline Reage, Adam Phillips, Montaigne, Laura Kipnis, Issa, Freud, Kawabata, Toni Bentley, Pessoa, Irving Goffman. *Humiliation*; *The Bedtrick*; *Advice on Dying*; *Objects of Desire*; *Night Games*; *Arousal*. Bringing five or six books at a time into the cottage to his study—selective reading, trolling for what will provoke him to ponder, react, elaborate. And what's on his mind? Oh, well: passion, etymology, aging, love, self-deception, lives in art, humiliation, received wisdom, ongoing presence of the dead, idioms, death, word-play. And the medium in which he'll work? Once again, the epigrammatic. It turns out his *Truth be Told*: New and Collected Premortems had left him hungry for more.

Such an odd form: to strive for compression, verbal surprise, paradox, shock, rueful acknowledgment, or revelation of moral blindness may elicit, exaggerate, one's own oddities. Make one too determined to implicate the reader, the writer. Through, or at the risk of, hyperbole, reductionism, unfairness. Doing so with dictionaries close at hand. Focusing, laser-like, on a single line—erotics of the irreducible. Or working on a tiny canvas, like the 1970s artist who painted imaginary postage stamps. Or hounding an emotion, backtracking all the way back to...root meaning, concealed impulse. Precluding, preempting, response. Such a pursuit requiring silence—writing time, reading time. Something long-gone about it, pre-modern. Connecting across centuries & tongues to, say, Martial, La Rochefoucauld, Lichtenberg: blood brothers; bad boys.

Frequently asked question: Does the epigrammist consider nothing sacred? Is he without scruple or restraint?

Answer: Ideally, yes. Nonetheless, the utterances of some kind souls can leave one...almost speechless. The Dalai Lama, for instance, writes that "when a person has achieved a high level of practice in motivation and wisdom, even the joining of the two sex organs...does not detract from the maintenance of pure behavior."

Picture the epigrammist at his desk, mulling this vision of realizing "the emptiness of inherent existence." Wishing he'd been able to quote the Dalai Lama to reluctant sweethearts when he was a teenager. Thought of just which ones might have tumbled to such suasion making him grin, but, oops, there's a knock-knock-knock at the study door. 碧琴 making her entrance, sitting on the writer's lap to be read to, hear this text's latest vituperation, condensation, contortion, calumny. Beautiful girl. Art; life.

(2008)

III

HESITATION MARKS
(2009)

The dash is used to denote a sudden change in the construction, a suspension of sense, an unexpected transition in the sentiment, a sudden interruption, or hesitation.

The New International Encyclopedia

...any cut or wound that is self-inflicted after a decision is made not to commit suicide, or...before the final cut that causes death.

Enotes.com

He was on top of her.
She was under appreciated.

Jealousy's geometry: no right triangles.

With “Fuck you,” the I is silent.
And well understood.

Desiring elective invisibility, in old age the secretive get part of their wish.

So intuitive, the old, certain something bad will happen soon.

Tango, envy: it takes two to.

On the other hand, the envious do manifest concern.

Less that he wanted a divorce, more that for his wife he wished a new husband.

Wife's pang before betraying her husband: pre-coital *tristesse*.

With performative verbs, the act's achieved in the saying:
"I quit," "War is declared," "Objection overruled."
A non-performative verb, on the other hand, is the kind of thing uttered by the man who says, "I'm going to fuck you," then fails to get it up.

'Senile libido.' Krafft-Ebing, in *Pyschopathia sexualis*, argued, "The manifestation of sexual instinct in old age is not in itself pathological." Though—you never know—it could be.

Hyperbolist, choking, superlative stuck in the craw of his better self.

Lifelong bachelor, he encourages his male friends' marital grousing, basks in their professed envy. Believes it when they say he's better off on his own.

Masturbating: beside herself with pleasure.

Masturbation, from the Greek, *mezea*, penises, and the Latin *turbare*, to disturb? Or from the Latin, *manu stuprare*, to defile with the hand? Manustupration: infrequently used term for the ubiquitous incessant.

She was the kind of hypocrite who regretted being one.

He was honest at heart, his hypocrisy pure pretense.

Hypocrisy: bad rep',
but not much worse than wanting something for nothing.

Five hundred fifty dollars/month. 'Abject poverty': what 16 million Americans live in, what the rest of us are able to live with.

"Self-made" multimillionaire railing against welfare fraud.
As if there's no such thing as social capital.

“When we start to die,” something he once thought began in old age.

“Had they only been loved,” something he once thought referred to the unhappy exception.

Born rich, decades of intimating he'd made his money at cards, currently sandbagging old age.

Support groups. As they say in French, *insupportable*.

Not just fat: full of himself.

The obese: couturiers doing not high fashion but *prêt à porter*.

Competitive senior citizen, still testosterone-poisoned, arguing his enlarged prostate's bigger than yours.

Old age. Indolent contemporary insinuating that, because you share a mutual inevitability, your lives were more or less the same.

"I just don't understand you," said a man who believed he understood himself.

Young biologist, just married, and, suddenly, avid library researcher. Female chimpanzees, he's learning, vocalize before and during penetration. Evolutionary advantage in screams and grunts: stimulating partners; blurring paternity to gain multiple protectors; allowing competing sperm access. So: young biologist, library, copulation calls. At home the night before, finally achieving orgasm by penetration, his bride had cried out, "I'm coming, everybody, I'm coming."

A YouPorn.com video: ‘Julie gets her ass reamed by an older man.’
[Duration: 22min 40sec; Views: 577,250 total (86,800 today);
Rating: 4.10/5.00 (890 ratings)...]
After the obligatory oral/genital/anal, the ‘older man’ ejaculates for the camera. Poignant for the godlike viewer: poor fellow won’t be doing such things much longer.

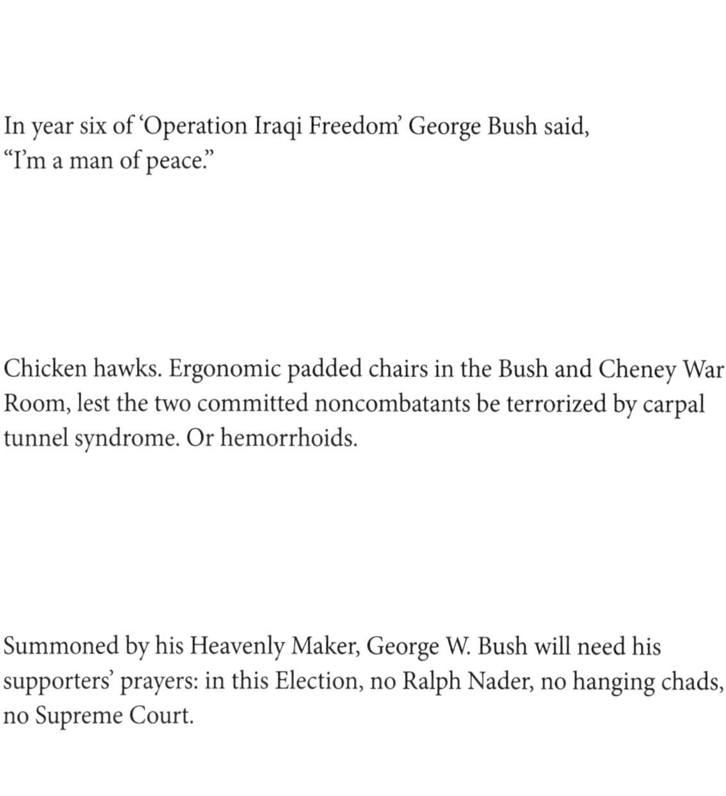

In year six of 'Operation Iraqi Freedom' George Bush said, "I'm a man of peace."

Chicken hawks. Ergonomic padded chairs in the Bush and Cheney War Room, lest the two committed noncombatants be terrorized by carpal tunnel syndrome. Or hemorrhoids.

Summoned by his Heavenly Maker, George W. Bush will need his supporters' prayers: in this Election, no Ralph Nader, no hanging chads, no Supreme Court.

Hypochondria: overkill.

Constipation: sit-down strike.

Misanthropy: overexposure.

'Double-teamed' by her boyfriend and her previous boyfriend.
Serial monogamy embracing multiple simultaneity.

Careerist word-workers watching what they say.
A prudence, a smarm, of poets.

New book of verse dedicated to her third husband, "Always."
Poetic license.

Too clever by half: his essays revealed character flaws his poems just managed to obscure.

Skilled writer, vivid imagination, but, still, unable to conceive there's a writer as good as himself.

Only the dead can be dead sure their love will never die.

Fungal or bacterial STDs (jock itch; gonorrhea): treatable, curable.

Bacterial STDs (genital herpes; warts): treatable, incurable.

Psychological STDs (jealousy): untreatable, incurable.

Diary—daily eulogy, and who could deliver it as well?
Something to live for.

‘Source amnesia,’ as, when you offer a sexual surprise to your lover, she asks, “Where did you learn that?”

The future. That which we can't yet remember.

The young: surprised when the body doesn't work.
The old: surprised when it does.

Undo.
Unravel.
Unlove.
Unfuck…

False modesty: truest thing about him.

1957. Mantra of a thirteen-year-old boy: “A breast in the hand is worth two in the bra.”

Suicide. By gun—ninety percent success rate;
by jumping from heights—thirty-three percent.
Choose one.

People contemplating suicide seek ease, speed, certainty.
And/or, a posthumous glimpse of some faces they'll be leaving behind.

Young woman, arching dolphin inked just above each breast. Tatts for tits.

“We’re going to be late,” the husband says, wife in front of mirror, outfits on bed, but for her the party began hours ago.

Inadequate collectors: found wanting.

In 'self-storage,' stuff left by shadows of their former selves.

Collectors: self, contained.

Pedophiles: *No Child Left Behind.*

Freud, no sexual intercourse after age forty.
Gandhi, celibate from age thirty-six on.
Draw the correct inference.

Freud, money as shit. Perhaps noting that the inherited rich avoid speaking about wealth to cover their assets.

Silent about inherited wealth, this capitalist.
Much gain, little venture.

The old: something's coming. One/one thousand, two/one thousand...

Old age: exit toll.

Not so much secretive as miserly, hoarding a wealth of information about the self.

At fifty, uncomfortable sharing, low need for affiliation:
only child become only adult.

Upscale restaurant, celebrating her birthday. Dining alone, a party of one.

How to tell she's your moral superior?
She'll let you know it.

Middle v. old age: out living v. outlived.

In the ballroom. She was old, Death too.
Experiencing a 'senior moment,' Death walked away.
But then, remembering what He was about, Death turned on His heel.
Asked her to dance.
Danced with her slow.

WHATEVER YOU SAY

The best epigrams, like the endings of great poems, shimmer and twist. Little is ended. There's much to think and feel. The rhetorical pleasure of an epigram may be its conclusiveness and concision, but the soul of its brevity is a long thoughtfulness.

WILLIAM MATTHEWS

I tell you after all that I do not hate mankind, it is *vous autres* who hate them because you would have them reasonable animals, and are angry for being disappointed.

JONATHAN SWIFT

Dubious—or squeamish—about the enterprise, some people inquire, "What motivates the epigrams?" Well...occasionally, they ensue from hearing a word or phrase as if for the first time, awakening to sound, layered meaning. Revealing or explicating latent or forgotten life in language. Surprise of achieved effect, illumination. Inevitably, written response entails shaping, radical compressing—the eros of craft. (But how much to pare away? Seneca and Chamfort labored to kill themselves; Ambrose Bierce disappeared, self-effaced.)

Sometimes, however, the impulse is a hunger to get at what's going on in our behavior, conviction it must be got at. A 'there is some shit we will not eat' kind of deal. Think of the word 'cant': inauthentic expressions of piety (from Latin, to chant, as in wheedling, importuning). On occasion, when cant provokes dismay, an epigram emerges. For instance: jacket copy from one of New Age exhorter Dr. Wayne Dyer's thirty books:

"Wayne spent one entire year reading, researching, and meditating on Lao-tzu's messages...and ultimately writing down these essays as he felt Lao-tzu wanted you to know them...As Wayne says, "This is a book that will forever change the way you look at your life... Writing this book changed me forever, too."

Forever? *Forever*? How clean the stables of such talk? Still, what else can a hero (try to) do? Satisfaction in the task, perceiving things previously unnamed/unseen/unacknowledged, pleasure in word play to express what's exposed. Corrected.

Finally, there's thrill in working so unmarketable a form. Think of, say, how skateboarding used to be, endless repetitions to achieve proficiency lacking dollar value in a culture that's all about dollars.

Still, there comes a time, and not just at night, when the epigrammist, age sixty-five, has had enough of distinctions/ precisions. Of purgatives/ assaults (Tom wounds all heels?), though as William Logan points out, "a poet of bilious emotion and narrow technique is better off writing epigrams, where dyspepsia is a recommendation, even an advantage." Seeking a different 'head,' as the hippies used to put it, the epigrammist remembers that one wouldn't want to live in a world of only the aphoristic, which, as Logan also argues, may prevent more thinking than it provokes. (Swift: in the mirror of satire "Beholders do generally discover every body's Face but their Own." Adorno: when love can only express itself by hatred for the inappropriate, one may come to resemble what he hates. William Matthews: "From Martial I learned foremost how important it is to find ways to be angry with human folly and failure and to be forgiving of it at the same time...") Chastened, the epigrammist is cheered to recall that God asked Adam and Eve, "Who told you you were naked?" though He might better have been forthcoming about His own attire.

All of which can give one pause. Suggest at least a momentary turning to, say, the open tunings of Hawaiian slack key guitar. A surrender to the lull of repose—hula of the palms in the trade winds. A closing of one's book.

Head on pillow. "It all happened for a reason," the epigrammist mutters, marveling that people can believe such things. And, drifting off to sleep, thinks "riddled with perfections." Expecting, when he wakes, to write it down.

(2009)

IV

FOREGONE CONCLUSIONS:
Equivoques, Aperçus, Spars & Catarrhs (2011)

Old man dozing in the sun. Acting his age.

Afternoon sex: what you get into with your eyes open.

She grew old, but not up.

She grew up, then down again.

He's a Dr. Jekyll who doesn't know about his Mr. Hyde.

Humans are mammals.
All mammals die.
Therefore all humans die.
Though surely there's the occasional exception.

Committed to the tropics, but far from family:
(warm) water is thicker than blood.

Eve, right after the apple: “Oh, Adam, he’s *way* too big for me.”

Older folk: explore's become deplore. Implore.

Jealousy: the two of you, the one of me.

Restaurant table for two,
husband and wife observing the marital vow of silence.

Monogamy, so you can each focus on food.

Species-of-one, the self, with its very own extinction event.

Your personal expiration date?
Blind…

He said "motherfucker" so often you had to take him at his word.

In defense of malice, it's not all aforethought.

Travel after death: where to; as who?

Old age: when yet another friend is former.

Self, older; winter, longer.

Begat, beset.
Beware, bemoan.
Bestow, betray.
Betroth, betwixt.
Beshat.
But not befuck.

His secrets, not kept but hoarded.

Dead, secrets were all he left behind.

Once drawn to a monastic vocation's silent chastity,
he instead achieved a spousal cold shoulder and unspoken
"No, not tonight."

Divorce: donated organs, rejected.

Religion-induced sanctimony—the gift divine.

Nocturia (Latin+Greek, night/urine): waking at night needing to pee. Drowning not in the ocean but in a piddle.

The last two centuries. From village community (*gemeinschaft*) to atomistic capitalism (*gesellschaft*).
From see to c.c.

She kept her secretiveness to herself.

She was so secretive people believed what she didn't tell them.

Their passionless marriage certified them as conventionally sexual.

Marriage: oft-belied promise not to find one's mate repugnant.

Cain and Abel, Joseph and his brothers, but *siblicide*,
not a word your parents taught you.

Sex researchers Meston & Buss write that "Smaller breasts are often more sensitive than larger ones."
Meaning God knows what She's doing (and how to play fair).

'Breast augmentation' surgery: three hundred thousand American women/year. Go on, go on, do the math.

Sleepless: nocternity.

Says the husband, much older than his wife, "You're my last love."
And he's hers too, so far.

But of course he had ethics! Like, say, the USA in Iraq.

Wise of her, to know more about others than about herself.

Reading others as like herself, she found them distasteful.

Rich: melancholy, fretful idler. Otherwise you might have wished him ill.

Inheritance at twenty-five, hasn't worked for years.
Anxious about inflation.
Suffers from insomnia, esophageal reflux, sciatica.
Old before his time.

Death's dissolution, not the preferred solution.

Senior discounts—for those going down for the count.

Not showing action, linking or copulative verbs establish a relationship between subject and complement.
To decide whether or not a verb is copulative, substitute am, is, or are.

Q: is fuck a copulative verb?

Occupational hazards.
Of marriage: rage—anger at the one to whom you are closest.
Of being single: depression—anger at the one to whom you are closest.

In an era of self-exposure, outing, and "transparency," he was still into manners, non-disclosure—discreet, reserved, self-contained. Not just old, then, but old fashioned.

Out of touch, out of sorts, out of control, out of it.
But then, out of need.

Seventy-five: archivist, apologist. Self-employed.

Seventy-five. Though he deems himself a Stoic, his perspective is merely age-inevitable.

When the rich say they're not, they mean not as rich as people they know.

Not needing, for many years, to earn a living, he worked hard on his philosophical pessimism.

Not a born fool, she became one.

All writing about the body: figurative.

"The question has to be asked..."
Or, maybe not.

He hadn't changed, it just took time to grasp what had stayed the same. And shouldn't have.

Child of the Sixties,"free spirit" and "anarchist," evader of draft/taxes/jury duty/matrimony. Now on Medi-Cal and saved, three times, by calling 911. At family gatherings, his siblings argue about whether or not to seat him with the grown-ups.

Living: death deferred. Not that Death defers.

Thinking/writing: vapor/paper.

She had a gift for making friends former.

Misanthropic fossil hunter, wishing humans mere impressions of themselves.

Misogyny, male loathing of an aspect of the self.

Hospital waiting room, the old. Waiting for...?

Package of the aging self. Mailed *Express*, *Fragile*, *Destination Unknown*.

‘Sexsomnia,’ a form of ‘parasomnia.’
Mind/body disconnect causing fondling or sexual assault while asleep?
Or mind’s morning-after story about what was done by body,
by mind and body, or
by two minds/two bodies.

He feared only those he feared understood him.

Amenable to being forthright, but bound by terms of a nondisclosure agreement signed with himself.

When not repeating itself, history stutters.

Footing the bill: no mean feat when the foot is bare.

He met a girl named Well Enough, which is why he never asked her out.

The man determined to avoid social pressure.
Cremated, the better part of him vanished into thin air.

Asked, six decades ago,"Where you goin'?" we kids replied, "Nowhere fast," a rejoinder one could live to regret.

Though the young tell their bodies what to do, the bodies of the old turn a deaf ear.

Old English *maeth*, skinning, mowing.
Aftermath, second mowing in the same season,
hence results, consequences.

The single-handed circumnavigator stayed in port, where
sex and (maybe) love were.
Lost at land.

Diary: gossip, closed circuit, cheek to cheek.

Parent/child. All about power: em-/disem-/over-.

Asked "Is narrative dead or dying?" author Bernard Malamud replied (testily),"It'll be dead when the penis is." For doctors, 'erectile dysfunction' portends cardio-vascular disaster. For patients, 'impotence' evokes regret (loss of colleague); relief (rescue from tormentor); rue (smoking, red meat & now this?); or, for literary types, the death of narrative.

Live and learn.
Relive and not learn.

Surprise, writer making the case for a style not his own.

Memoirist on book tour,
yet again retelling
the story of the story of her life.

When painter Mark Rothko said “Silence is so accurate,” silence is what he broke.

Eat much/stay trim? Fat chance.

To confound: not helping you to find.

That pretty co-ed's wasting herself on some young fool,
thinks the old fool.

He found it harder to distinguish between things intended and things done.

Sandwiched between in and of, spite lost its venomous ill will.

The idea of her? Worse than the reality.

Aesthetes without an art have a high opinion of opinion.

Old age: when you know the game is up.

Suicide: when you know the game is up and want to end it.

If the old ask, "Which way?" graciously explain, "Dead ahead."

Clear of various maladies, he felt like himself again.
Which, despite character flaws, he preferred to not feeling like himself.

Under the weather, and suicidal,
undertaking the question of whether or not.

Domestication: to breed in captivity.
Dogs, ducks.
Silk moths, cows.
Llamas, goldfish.
Husbands, wives.

End-of-life realization:
too worn out to hate your enemies,
too worn out to make peace.

What to do when others ask too much of you?
Wait ’til your golden years, when, odds are, they’ll come ’round less often.

Sir Thomas Wyatt's "They flee from me that sometime did me seek..."
Poetical self-pity: late adolescent, and, not infrequently,
(warning) sign of old age.

‘Twin’ mattress? Siamese, maybe.

"It's *my* life," he said. *His* death, too.

Conclusion of one's life? Foregone.

DEATHLESS DAYS OF OLD

Dear Reader: How are you? Fine, I trust. Long life, good health. And me? As of this writing, all's well, thank you. Sixty-six, bit the worse for wear, but, as the idiom goes, got my "whole life ahead of me." Though there are days when I feel "like death warmed over," still, we're only talkin' ripe or very ripe (v. overripe or rot). Not "done fer," as movie cowboys used to say, but I do have reason to sense my time is coming. Cross my heart, hope t' die.

What to make of this foregone conclusion? Well, one can commit more epigrams. Recently, introducing himself by email, aphorist Yahia Lababidi wrote me, "It is a curious compulsion to try to condense so much thought and observation in such little space...to discover another practitioner of this brief art is like discovering another member of an endangered species." To which I replied—succinctly enough, I hope—that it *is* a curious compulsion. And that perhaps our odd species should be...even more endangered.

I was thinking, you see, of a recent video made by Andrea Young, also publisher of *Hesitation Marks*, my book of the epigrammatic. In Andrea's *Interrogations of Thomas Farber*, one of my interviewers is a twenty-four-year-old Danish woman, visiting "student and humanitarian" eager to meet people "I can look to who changed the world." Such an implausibly fresh, implausibly earnest soul! Scrupulously tactful. Pretty, too.

Severely tempted, but remembering we were on camera to commit Art—and/or sobered by her guileless "What can I learn from you?"—I forbade myself bad-boy poet Frederick Seidel's "hunger for younger." Really, what could this lovely young woman learn from me? Manfully, high-mindedly,

I spoke of truth in language, usefulness of self-knowledge. Almost instantly exhausted, however, by this effort to be good, I confided that at her age I wouldn't have liked the epigrams. Too dark. I might have added, but didn't, that self-knowledge wasn't then my goal: sexual hunger and conviction of myself as jeopardized hero were my imperatives, storyline.

Toward the end of our videotaped conversation, when this improbably good young woman asked the provenance of *Hesitation Marks*' title, I stroked right index finger as razor blade across veins of left wrist, demonstrating one of the meanings. Seeing her dismay, I urged her to keep the epigrams "for later." And, I said, laughing, half-ruing the syllables as they reached my ear, "Save them for marriage." Not for the first time, putting words in my own mouth.

Free from dissimulation as this ingénue seemed, artless as I believed (wanted to believe?) her to be (she had a "boyfriend," whatever he entailed), she and I were not utterly different. Her impulse to save the world was a refusal to reconcile with things as they are. Though my kind of wordworker, reveling in inflammatory, hyperbolic illumination, has little interest in making peace, there is the impulse to set things straight. And, more, insistent linking of the apparently incompatible, also a form of reconciliation. Late in life, George Carlin wrote of his one-man routines, "What may sound to some like anger is really nothing more than sympathetic contempt." I myself prefer the notion of tough love. In the poem *Circe's Power*, by Louise Glück, the *Odyssey*-famous sorceress says: "I never turned anyone into a pig/Some people are pigs; I make them/ Look like pigs."

"What do you see in books?" an amiable cocaine dealer, idly curious, asked me in the 1980s. About epigrams, I might have cited Alex Mawyer: "There's much to be said for them." For instance: epigrammist as stand-up comic playing a tough room. Epigrams overstated and concise, exhibitionistic with Olympian detachment, precluding demurral, arguing aspect as whole, aspiring to the oracular. Written, Clifton Fadiman argued,"not to improve ourselves but to feel the pleasure that comes of recognizing how unimproved (or, still more gratifying, how unimprovable)" others are. The risk, aphorist Don Paterson self-pleasuringly self-deprecates, being that all axioms sound as if "delivered by the same disenfranchised, bad-tempered minor deity." Half-true, though I hear more, and not just love of language—the anger's alloyed with grief. Camus wrote that in a time of pestilence "there are more things in men to admire than to despise," an affirmation epigrammists may have trouble achieving.

Forty years ago, on short notice, I taught a college course in argumentation and rhetoric. Reading about suasive language, a step ahead of my students, I learned "I love you" might be arguing, "Love is good/I love you/Therefore you should love me." Scales fell from my eyes. Thus, decades later, the epigrammatic as an effort to unmask what's concealed, unacknowledged. Recently, commenting on my reference to a youporn.com video in *Hesitation Marks*, an old friend, lawyer in a conservative small town, thought it brave of me to reveal I must have watched the video. Just part of my job, I explained, to talk about our lives-as-lived if and as I could. There's also the 'senile sublime': late work of older writers, intelligible or not, but pared way, way down, ever less in need of pleasing or appeasing others.

Fragments. Tony Hoagland writes that "Since the early days of modernism, there has been an argument about how little a poem could contain before too many of the burdens of meaning passed from writer to reader." For sure, the epigrammatic tests that boundary. Under-tellings, intimated or hidden back-stories, "fracture and breakage." There's also dispute about the politics of fragment—is narrative's coherence only false promise, placating in the service of power? For writers at work, such questions may not be primary: much comes simply in release from the physical burdens of extended prose. Maxine Hong Kingston, forswearing novels in favor of poetry, says henceforth she will be not workhorse but skylark. For the aging writer, in any case, the epigrammatic may simply contain all that need/should/can be said.

Humor. Writing and rewriting these spars and catarrhs, I sometimes laughed. Because of wordplay, of course. But also because I was turning moral blindness, often my own, into recognition of the distance between error and self-knowledge, self-image and fact. If the epigrammist appears to presume himself superior to others, of course he's there in all he perceives. As, when children, insulted, we'd retort,"Takes one to know one."

Last thoughts.

1. Sometimes it's just sound and a smile: "I'm partial to ugly," writes Cecil Giscombe.
2. Sometimes shocking fact—Norman Mailer, dying. Toothless, literally.
3. Or, sometimes, things people say, like the fellow selling "healing erotic touch" on Craigslist."They aren't paying me for sex," he told an interviewer. "They are paying me to leave."

(2011)

V

PARTING SHOTS:
Alerts, Rebuffs, Cold Comforts, Sequiturs & Amends (2013)

Yet in other ways the dead gain by death.

NICHOLSON BAKER, *U & I*

Second childhood: when you get to change your own diapers.

Breast, proffer of a nipple. Child's-play at nearly any age.

Children learn elephants never forget.
Grownups learn women never forget.

Messianic about marriage; rebukes former fellow debauchees:
no monogamist like a reformed cunt-hound.

Though it brings tears to his eyes to tell people his wife's his "queen,"
he's consorting in other kingdoms.

Eyes downcast, old man shuffles past.
Mutters "Morning" as if there's a U after the O.

Street person's "Spare change?"
Tyranny of the disadvantaged?
Fair question?

"Compassion fatigue:" corollary of American exceptionalism.

Old friends, estranged. The black magic of grudge, grievance, umbrage, pique. Bygones no longer bygones. *Were* alchemized into *never was.*

Dog's best friend, attentive, plastic bag in hand.
Fido imagining a bathroom door.

Dog's best friend, attentive, plastic bag in hand.
Fido thinking "coprophiliacs."

"But I love my wife," he protests, as if love has never coerced.

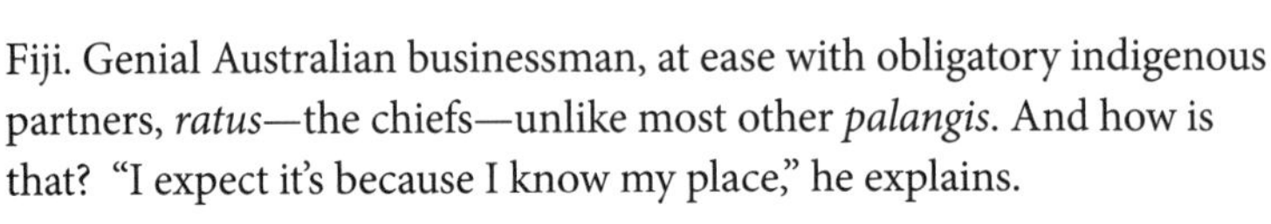

Fiji. Genial Australian businessman, at ease with obligatory indigenous partners, *ratus*—the chiefs—unlike most other *palangis*. And how is that? "I expect it's because I know my place," he explains.

"Hawaii's a further California," argues the former Angeleno, which may be why he drinks so much.

In Hawai'i for a one-week spiritual retreat, texting friends back home she feels its divine kundalini power, is opening herself to new dimensions. Should she extend her stay, she'll also learn that there she's *haole*, with all the karma that entails.

His jealousy made his wife's former lovers the story of her life. Their life, too.

Wife, raging, husband's "rancid" gym gear on clean bedspread. Marital bedroom; putrescence.

Old man, young woman, plunging décolletage. Something to live for.

Dazzled, each day shimmering, glorious, beyond believing.
That is, he must be getting old.

Neoteny: prolongation of juvenile characteristics into maturity, evolutionarily good for the species, though many Attention-Deficited young males, safe in parental nest, seem genetically programmed for video gaming, unpaid sex, and Internet porn. Given such boy toys & Peter Pans, lacking mates for propagation, young women turn to… toy-dogs. Also neotenous, but on leash. Collared.

No uniforms, no dictators?

The old have two questions:

1. "Do you think I always looked like this?"
2. "Do you think you'll never look like this?"

Restaurant table for two, husband and wife conversing without eye contact, Smartphones in hand. Smart indeed: release from the marital pretense of undivided attention.

Clueless, she lacked requisite self-loathing.

Strategy for dying?
Since this too shall pass, just wait it out.

July 4. The rockets' red glare, our virtual Shock and Awe. Meanwhile, celebrating, what can we buy? A Cadillac Escalade? Room for 8 adults. Supple leather-trimmed, 14-way power-adjustable front seats with memory settings, elegant French-stitched seams. Premium 10-speaker Bose® 5.1 surround sound system. Leather-and-wood-trimmed steering wheel. Power-adjustable, heated...Oh, America the insatiable! Engorged, gorging. Land of the free, though no doubt there'll be a price to pay.

Yoga teachers having sex with students!
But, still, no mention of auto-fellatio.

Older author, writer's block, endeavoring to rewrite his will.

"Elimination period," between illness' onset and first insurance payment.
Shorter wait/higher premium, but better than elimination, period.

When she told him French-kissing's repugnant,
he held his tongue.
Bit it.

Late marriage, young wife. Some day she'll be half his age.

Beach, bikini bottoms barely covering genitals, anus, perineum.
G-strings, C-strings, V-strings, *hilo dental* (Spanish: dental floss).
Artifice inveigling you to imagine yourself next to next to nothing.

Compare+contrast: thongs, the epigrammatic.

Obese gourmand, unforced overfeeding.
Cooking his own goose?
Or, artisinal high liver, cultivating his *fois gras.*

Landlocked, drowning. Saved by warm ocean.

Old age: short pier, long walk.

Nearly-former spouses, $200,000 to $500-per-hour "Family Court" attorneys arguing who's more unfit. Funds finally depleted, joint procreators achieve (the inevitable) joint custody of their beloved child. Divorce, proceeding…

End of life: "The last woman I slept with" becomes
"The last woman he slept with."

Money worries?
Nope: free of care, money talks, laughs at your expense.

The "liberal" journalist who championed war on Iraq. Five years later, a hedged mea culpa. *Seppuku* pending.

Life's a party. It's late. The old, overstaying their welcome.

If someone says "Mind you," mind you never mind.

In the agnostic's afterlife,
you may or may not get free of your own worst enemy.

Seven decades before, he'd wondered what he'd be when he grew up.

Old age: when no one can save you.

VI

AFTERWORD:
A MAN AND AN EPIGRAM WALK INTO A BAR

by Laura Glen Louis

Twenty years. Four hundred epigrams. A lot of compression. Born of Farber's self-proclaimed mania, this *oeuvre* has been nothing if not a tremendous labor of love. *I attend. I inquire. I probe. I dare. I reflect.* And: *I refute—silence,* that is. Behind all of which is Farber's favorite dis-apologia: *Fuck'em if they can't take a joke.*

Farber likens epigrams to prime numbers. Singular and irreducible, prime numbers are defined as those whose only two factors are 1 and itself. It's a unique pairing, with 1 ever the common denominator. So, where is the 1 in these epigrams if not — the author? His fingerprints are all over this crime scene. We're talking high velocity. Up close. *Bada bing.*

> Sex: what puts you in contact with people you might otherwise never know. (p. 11)
>
> My accountant's wife, #2: she's come to believe she was a Native American in a previous life. Before the white man's smallpox, she means. (p. 25)
>
> False modesty: the writer enraged Toni Morrison's won the Nobel Prize, but unable to come up with the name of someone he'd prefer. (p. 19)

But, also, silencers:

> Spacious bedroom. Room for misunderstanding. (p. 75)
>
> He'd grown afraid of winter. (p. 30)
>
> Epitaph: SEE YOU SOON. (p. 99)

Primes? Most of us can rattle off a few (our brains seize up around 37, 41) , and assume that surely they will run out. But no, they are infinite in number. Without end. So, epigrams. Limitless in possibility. Also, not limited to those words on the page. When spot on, epigrams reverberate, like a super tsunami. Long after we're gone. (To paraphrase Aristotle: Art endures.) Do I find 5683 as elegant a prime as 7? No. But both are exquisitely themselves and each is partnered to 1, that indefatigable, omnipresent, *cruising-to-infinity-hooking-up-with-ever-more-primes* 1.

A kind of Casanova of numbers, even more promiscuous than the towering star Farber slams with:

> Wilt Chamberlain's "20,000" lovers. Yo, Wilt: Names? Birthdays? (p. 59)

in which the *Yo, Wilt* delivers sly levity while sticking in the shiv. Yes, a preoccupation with sex and death. Eros. Thanatos.

> Some life forms never have sex, die, they say, only from external hazards. Life forms that do have sex always die. (p. 159)

Life forms that never have sex? What's that? I think oceanographer Sylvia Earle said that bacteria will survive even should all other life die out. As for the rest of us, we might argue to get it (sex), and get lots of it, since we are going to die anyway. We're just blips. Then, stepping back, isn't there something to be admired about irony and paradox? Something miraculous about death? Would you prefer immortality as bacteria, or a relatively short blast as bird, feline, or even human, pen in hand, or some other phallus of choice? Afraid of dying = afraid of living? Yes, yes, easy for me to say. Farber stands between me and silence.

> Turning fifty. Avoiding one's older friends.
> Lest what's happened to them prove contagious. (p. 9)

> Old age: when no one can save you. (p. 336)

Unsparing? Consider this from Farber's meditation *On Water*. Suva, Fiji. Outdoor weekend market, all manner of edible marine life splayed out for purchase, from octopus to parrotfish.

> And turtles... A very large one on its back, the lower shell, the plastron, already cut away, turtle being slowly, deliberately, butchered out while still alive, great heart still beating, pumping as the turtle urinates, urinates again, shell now a bowl for its own blood.... I turn away from this perfunctory but merciless slaughter. And turn back again to watch. And turn away again.
> (pp. 138-139, *On Water*, The Ecco Press, 1994)

The horror. Author makes himself look. He thinks about it, dreams about it, wakes writing about it. Lorrie Moore, her baby in and out of hospital with a Wilms tumor (kidney cancer), managed later to subsume the experience into a work of fiction: The Mother holding it together, barely, moving in the fog of disbelief, impotence and massive fear, The Husband saying, "Take notes. We are going to need the money." This is what writers do, go into the blind cave even though Cyclops is host. This is the way we earn our way home.

Here's Farber, Boston, age ten, from the essay "Testaments & Mea Culpas," 2005:

> ...we also well knew what it was to be "crying mad," to
> turn away from the sight of tears in others. For the grownup
> epigrammist, then, perhaps the motto should be "No flinch-
> ing." Something we kids used to say, in moments long ago
> lost, when it was again our turn to strike the blow. (p. 105)

What an about face those last six words. Not "our turn to take it," but "our turn to dish it out." Still, if the author is ever over the top in sticking it in the most putrid part of someone else's foibles, neither is he letting himself off the hook. Observer, even of himself. Perhaps firstly of himself.

> "My wife," he frequently says, even to those who know her
> proper name. (p. 57)

Need to declare the (unearned?) possessive (kin to "My son, the doctor")? Charmed by it? Need to test the reality, to see if it will hold? For husband and/or wife? Or, just the sweet wonder of commitment, and what commitment asks? This epigram was written in 1998, about a decade before Farber himself finally renounced a self-professed promiscuous bachelorhood (*Yo, Tom!*) and married; and for the first months, as if in self-fulfilling prophecy, he ever referred to his beloved as "My wife, my wife." Fast forward to 2012, from *Parting Shots*:

> Messianic about marriage; rebukes former fellow debauchees:
> no monogamist like a reformed cunt-hound. (p. 304)

But neither does the (married) eye stop looking, assessing, appreciating, tripping:

> Compare + contrast: thongs, the epigrammatic. (p. 324)

Still later:

> End of life: "The last woman I slept with" becomes
> "The last woman he slept with." (p. 329)

Underlying every inquiry and compression is Farber's love of words and wordplay.

> Hypochondria: overkill. (p. 190)

> Not just fat: full of himself. (p. 184)

> Children learn elephants never forget.
> Grownups learn women never forget. (p. 303)

Funny, right? Now look at this:

> Thinking/writing: vapor/paper. (p. 264)

Oh, my. Every artist knows this one. But look also at the parallel structure that makes this such a well-cut gem: the gerunds on the verso side of the equation, giving up their tinkering rhyme; then listen to the plosives of the "p"s on the recto side, which evoke puffs, as in *Poof! Gone* —if you don't get up out of bed and write those suckers down.

Writers have words. That's all we have. How we combine these words, juxtapose them, allude with, and to, them, exclude them altogether, coin new words, bring out new lights, refractions, reflections—words are our paint, our music, our song. *Word*'s root? From my *American Heritage*: wer-5: derivatives include *word*, *verb*, *adverb* (modifier of verbs), *proverb* (brisk, terse, and true), verve (vigor, spirit, style), and irony (saying the opposite of what you mean, *with effect*). Epigrams, in spades.

"Beneath contempt." Down there somewhere. (p. 49)

Aesthetes without an art have a high opinion of opinion. (p. 286)

Pedophiles: *No Child Left Behind* (p. 208)

You may be tempted to skip. Flip through, blindly poke your finger on a page for no other reason than you like the way the line basks in the tundra of white space. Or, you might feel compelled to just put the book down. Farber has spent a lifetime suffering no fools, but that doesn't mean you have to suffer along with him. He's quick to own, again and again, the form's bleakness.

Do we need such honesty, such a polished mirror held up to our less noble selves? Do we need these reminders of what we are capable of? Do we need Tom Hagen's offer no one can refuse, bloody, in our beds? Nick Ut's photo: Kim Phúc running naked the streets of Trang Bang, her back on fire from napalm? Or the Munch-like silent scream of the boy closest to us? Do we need burnished into our souls what Iris Chang brought back from Nanking, and what she gave of herself to do so? James Dickey's *Deliverance*? Wilfred Owen's lines set by Benjamin Britten in his *War Requiem*? Or Mahler's *Kindertotenlieder*? Can we listen without crying? Do we need to have our hearts broken? Well, only if we want to feel. The breaking of our hearts corroborates that we are sentient. No great love without great loss.

Dylan Thomas ends his masterful poem with this couplet, "Do not go gentle into that good night. / Rage, rage against the dying of the light." His father dying, Thomas imploring, that we fail to see what is grand before us, that wisdom goes unheeded is no reason to stop trying. In five tercets and the concluding quatrain, these two lines alternate in repetition no fewer than four times each. Or, of the 19 lines, nearly half of them beg an open-eyed living to the very last breath, their incantatory repetition a *cri de coeur*.

One of Farber's friends, "a very goodhearted poet" said, upon reading *The Price of the Ride*, "At the end of that road is silence." Farber: "There are worse things than silence." Apathy. Ignorance. Dishonor. Pick one. Yet, not to say the hard truth—is *that* not is the fastest shortcut to silence?

Read these piths for Farber's spin on, among the vast array of human frailties: jealously, false modesty, secrecy, marriage, adultery, betrayal, aging, dying, death, the self-delusion about the same, and what it means to be *preposterous*. (p. 95) Compression, as a life pursuit. There's a certain samurai nobility.

Consider, now, two fine stories by Irwin Shaw: "The Eighty Yard Run"; and "The Girls in Their Summer Dresses"—titles alone that are longer than some of these epigrams—each a lament to lost youth, lost opportunities, sentiments etched by these few quick lines keen with Farber's judicious use of adjective in achieving the above, and more: mood, setting, resignation, poignancy, in possibilities pondered and possibilities discarded. Bravura compression:

> A man in middle age sitting in an outdoor café. Two young women passing his table, walking faster than he thinks he'd be able to run after them. (p. 8)

This is where Farber's epigrammatic journey began twenty years ago, with wistfulness in middle age. Then he took off his gloves and went *mano a mano* with his own mortality.

—Laura Glen Louis is the author of *Talking in the Dark* and *Some, like elephants.*
Visit www.lauraglenlouis.com

ABOUT THE AUTHOR

Recipient of Guggenheim, National Endowment, Rockefeller, Fulbright, and Dorothea Lange–Paul Taylor fellowships, Thomas Farber is the author of many works of fiction, creative nonfiction, and the epigrammatic.

Visit www.thomasfarber.org